CW01312983

Other Duties; Not Assigned

A Guide to Teaching

By

Darcel Pledge

ISBN: *9798596475296*

Dedication

I want to dedicate this book to all my past classroom Princes & Princesses that have ever set foot in the Queendom. Without you, I would not have had all these funny memories, experiences, and growth as an educator. Thank you! I wish you all the best!

~Queen Pledge

Introduction

"And other duties as assigned."

It was not until I became an educator that this phrase became a recurring theme in my day-to-day life as a teacher. While I knew this meant teachers will do more than teaching academics in their workday; that phrase took on a whole new meaning as the years went on. I learned that other duties assigned could mean recess duty, covering a teaching partner's class that was sick or had to leave early, helping in the lunchroom, field trips, helping students leave for the end of the day, and MANY more tasks assigned outside of the typical workday. I got used to "And other duties as assigned". They tended to be the technical details; sometimes spur of the moment that many of the educators I knew had no problem stepping up to lend a hand with because it would help the greater good of our system aka our school building. I was cool with "And other duties assigned". It became natural and as the years went by that "And other duties assigned" was a package deal with being an educator. However, what brought me the most growth and stretched my thinking the most was the "other duties NOT assigned". I learned that those duties were not technical. They were duties that dealt with being open to understanding each person, building relationships, showing empathy, thinking of equity, and finding unique & engaging ways to reach students. The things our teacher prep programs often do not have the full ability to prepare us for. Those "other duties NOT assigned" pushed me, humbled me, and kept my focus on what was most important: my students, their learning, & the environment I prepared for them each day to be successful. I do not consider myself an expert by any means, but I do know I put a lot of hard work into my teaching role. I focused on making my learning environment feel like a second home and it was that aspect I enjoyed the most during my years in the classroom. I invite you to come along as I give some tips, tricks, & confessions on how these other duties not assigned helped this second career educator navigate the waters of teaching.

Contents

Chapter 1
Oh B.O.Y (Beginning of Year)

The Nuts & Bolts

Imagine the last time you had a fresh start. It may have brought you excitement, joy, fear, or anxiety. Possibly a mix of all these emotions at once. Now imagine reliving that fresh start year after year. This is a recurring reality for every educator. For me, this was the time of year I thought about the most. I would spend weeks in the summer planning out the intricate details of my classroom theme to plan for this fresh start. The goal was to hook new students or live up to the expectation of incoming siblings or students who may have had a taste of what my classroom (The Queendom) had to offer. Full confession, I'd say my final year "Bitmoji Queendom" theme was my favorite. However, is a theme all you need to start the year off? Is it worth spending summer vacation to only have your theme figured out? I would have to say no. While setting up the environment was a critical part in preparing me for a new year, it was one piece of the pie. My mindset was that I had to get my students to buy into school and working hard to learn the skills necessary for the year and their lives moving forward. It was my job to find ways to make their work engaging and keep them interested in my business of teaching. So, while the cute posters, stickers, and the room layout were there; it was nothing without a genuine purpose of how I wanted it to serve and prepare my kiddos to be able to do the work I was presenting before them. I found that from day one I needed to figure out my students as they were figuring out the lay of the land I had created. Every year, I used that first week as an opportunity to collect information about each student. I often repeated to my students throughout the year, "You don't have to like me or anyone in this room for that matter, but in this classroom, you will respect me, and your classmates and I will do the same". This meant I needed to know what respecting my students looked like. Which was always my first tier of building classroom community. I wanted to know what students expected of me first before letting them know what I expected of them. When asking students what respect from their teacher looked and sounded like to them, I often got responses such as:

- *"A teacher who doesn't yell."*
- *"Having a private conversation instead of calling them out in front of everyone."*
- *"Doing fun activities."*
- *"Not punishing the whole class for things only a few people are consistently doing."*
- *"Hearing them out in a situation vs taking one person's word."*

These are just a few examples, but I often found their requirements of me and what they considered as showing respect to them did not have anything to with the academic side of what I was teaching them. It was how I would handle mistakes should they make them. This type of vulnerability so early in the school year showed me just how much these students had carried year to year from experiences with other teachers. I felt that I owed it to them to break whatever notion they had ingrained in their head about what a partnership with their teacher truly looked like. I was not their parent, and I did not want to come across in that way. I wanted to be viewed as an adult that they could respect and could tell genuinely cared about them, their learning, and their future. So, guess what I did? I had a morning meeting the very next day after getting their responses to prove to them that their words meant something and carried weight with me. I committed and set an expectation for myself to not do the things they had communicated to me. However, for our year to work we would need to have a partnership that also meant they would need to adhere to my expectations to make our learning environment a calm place for everyone to function and learn. My expectations of them mirrored what they had requested of me. For them to respect me with their tone, words, and actions and trust me to figure out and get to the bottom of situations that may frustrate them. That I would communicate with students directly if they were not following directions vs calling them out. Some fun was in the plan if they could handle it. Ultimately, I wanted my students to be open to learning, making mistakes, and being reachable from both an academic and social-emotional standpoint. In a nutshell, that was always my priority that first week of the school year along with teaching the normal routine and procedures typical in any school building. Academics easily came in via games and quick stamina-building activities to see their basic knowledge, effort, and engagement in core content areas. By focusing on building relationships first, I learned what my students liked and incorporated those things immediately to again prove that I was listening and trusted them to show me the same respect.

Communication

Communication with my students was critical from day one. I am speaking of the communication related to what our days would entail and what all our jobs were to make our days together a success. Having an agenda present was the core way to help my students understand our daily schedule. Outside of knowing what was going on throughout our day, students need to know how they can communicate with their teachers. They will not know when the appropriate times are to ask for help unless they are taught this expectation. I always had a few systems in place and taught them how to communicate with me appropriately. My students could usually do an "I wish my teacher knew" form, write me a letter, or leave a post-it note on my desk if they needed to talk. They also knew that if it were work time and I was not teaching a group they could ask to talk to me if it was urgent. I would often try to eat lunch with as many kids as possible the first two weeks of school and just talk to them. I found these lunches to be more informative for me to hear more about them personally. I would also use this time to get a feel for how students interacted with their peers. I wanted to learn which of their mannerisms they were entering my room with from the start vs traits they would later pick up in the year from peers. These lunch discussions would also circle back to us talking again about what they would like to see throughout the year. As they may be more comfortable sharing days later vs the first day.

There are so many "technical" things you can do at the start of the year. When I think of the beginning of the year, I think of that first month of school and all the things that are critical for students to learn to do while having other kids around them. It is important to consider who is entering your class and plan for how to accommodate those students. Now, will you be able to make every single student happy with your classroom system? Probably not, but if you are trying and finding ways to communicate with them to bring some of their desires into play, I'd say that's a great achievement. Too often educators want to jump into content when their class may not even know how to sit on the carpet properly to learn. I learned early on, it is ok to take the time to reteach, reinforce, reward, and reflect on the structural elements of school. The more consistent you are in the beginning with doing this, the less time it will take the remainder of the year. This will pay off in the long run I promise!

Ok, so I am feeling like you are ready to start your year! Having been in your place, I also remember reading all these books only to find that no one gave me concrete details on what exactly to do. So, wait no more, on the next page I am sharing what a typical beginning of year morning looked like in the Queendom. The morning was critical because it set the tone for how the rest of the day would go. Was it always perfect? No, but was it always planned? Yes! In my mind as a new teacher, I welcomed a calm morning vs having the whole day being chaotic. Structure and routine proved to be a benefit in my classroom.

First Morning in the Queendom (Elementary Edition)

Arrival

• A full schedule with times on the board under the set agenda spot, along with a morning message presented on the smart board letting students know directions, voice level expectations, and what to do when they were finished with their morning work.
• Student's desks/learning space had a chair, a pencil, and their morning work. The morning work was always some sort of getting to know you page with a crossword or something fun on the back (2 sides to give you a chance to handle anything unexpectedly- trust me, there's usually something).
• Once the bell rang, I'd be standing by the door to greet students; I would let them come in and just watch how the whole transition went down (keeping in mind everything from how they entered, how long

it took them to find their space, voice level, interactions with peers, etc.).
• At this point after lunch count and the Pledge, it was officially go time!
• Next, we would move to the carpet for our first-morning meeting (with no set seating arrangement, this allowed me to see who were friends with who based on who they sat by.
• After welcoming them to the class & school year, I'd normally ask a question to get them talking. Something as simple as "What was your favorite part of summer?". Give them think time, have them share with a partner or small group near them, then allow them to volunteer to share with the whole class.
• Once we got acquainted, this was my opportunity to give them instant feedback from that small amount of time in the morning. I would always start with what they did well (**"THANK YOU ALL FOR COMING IN SO CALMLY AND QUIETLY, GETTING TO YOUR SEATS, READING THE BOARD TO FIGURE OUT YOUR TASK"** etc.). By giving them early praises, it allowed me to let them know they had already mastered some of the expectations for the school that we would be talking about throughout the week and

that we were already ahead of the game. The praise would be followed up with whatever the school incentive may be (tickets, class paws, etc.).
• Briefly, I would comment on the other things we would practice and go over that day. Not to put them down or call them out, but to set up in their minds that we were going to be learning a routine or procedure for whatever those things were. These were usually actions, transitions, or behaviors that may not have gone so well (i.e. running into the room, coming in loudly, disrupting others during morning work, etc.).
• I'd throw in some more get-to-know-you questions and then I'd tell them that we would be switching gears so that I can learn more about them and what things might make their year more successful and enjoyable. At this point if the transitions needed practice, this was an opportunity to correct that behavior. Letting them know I'd set a timer to see how quickly and calmly they could get back to their seat without talking, get out a piece of paper and begin writing me a note about their needs and wants for the school year.

- We'd continue working on that transition time for the rest of the day. If it took 2 minutes for everyone to get to where they needed to be starting out, the goal would be to time this all day and at the end of the day give them feedback on how they improved this throughout the whole day. Also, what the expectation is moving forward if they didn't hit it. Most of my classes could easily get from the carpet to their seats or line within 30 seconds or less.

The rest of the day would be dedicated to teaching and practicing the necessary expectations that would help them not question what was required on day two and moving forward. The goal was patience, positivity, praise, and reflection throughout that first day. My highlight at the very end of the day was letting them know all the positives I had witnessed in our time together. They needed to know that they did a great job lining up, entering the room, working with a partner, or maintaining an appropriate voice level. I wanted them to understand these were the great choices I would be looking for all year. Consistency is the key! Don't shy away from addressing unexpected behaviors early on.

A Few Other Helpful Beginning of Year Tips

Figure out a reward system that you can utilize. This could be school tickets or something you've created to track how students are doing with adjusting back to the classroom. Actively use that reward system to reward individual behavior and whole class behavior within a short time frame of the year starting. I would usually try to have one whole class celebration by the end of that first week if they earned it.

Come up with a classroom contract that specifically states what your agreed upon classroom rules are. Community circle time is a great place to decide on at least 5 rules that would help the year run smoothly. I would put these rules on a class contract and list the positive consequences that could occur from them following the rules and the negative consequences that could happen if the rules were broke.

Fully plan to teach students and have them practice all the things you feel are pertinent factors in having a successful year. Even things that seem small such as pencil sharpening or using a class library book.

Develop class jobs and slowly roll them out. Your students will want to help, and I found a lot of my leaders by giving some helpful tasks. I would have a designated pencil sharpener, paper collector, chair stacker / unstacker, library organizer, lunch count taker during morning work are some examples.

Have a technology resource wall where you can display all the logins and passwords they will need.

Try to make a positive contact home for each student within the first couple of weeks of school. This could be a personal note, phone call, or email, but find something!

Chapter 2
Where my P.O.M.S at? (Parents of My Students)

Breaking the Ice

My first couple of years I struggled with finding the balance on when, how, or even why I should contact parents or guardians. Essentially, I had some textbook scenarios of when parent contact was warranted (back-to-school night, conferences, class event sign-ups, and the dreaded consequence contact). However, just like my classroom; I wanted to make this my own and find a way to at least keep parents consistently informed throughout the year. Being a parent entering the education field, I was able to use myself as a guide to know what I would want to know about my child in school. I eventually put the following things in place and continued to make changes as each year went on. Ultimately each year in the Queendom, parents were guaranteed the following:

All About the student/Parent Preferences

I found a basic student info page on the teacher lifeline site teacherspayteachers.com. I then tweaked this page to ask the right questions that I needed to know. I always made sure to have the sheet ready to go for the supply drop-off/back-to-school night. This was usually a sure-fire way I could guarantee I would meet and see almost all my student's parents or guardians at least once. I would have them fill out the information they thought would be helpful for me to know about their student, even what triggered their child and ways to calm them down. Also, what their preferences were as far as me contacting them. They could choose to be contacted electronically, by text, via a physical document, or select all options. I would keep this completed page in my teacher binder all year and refer to it as needed.

Website

My class website was a free version from weebly.com. It had the basics about me, expectations, grade-level content we would cover and a spot with my contact info or they could fill out a form on the website directly to reach me. I had a page dedicated to what our week consisted of. I did a daily breakdown that included everything about school and classroom news, events, and homework due. I also made sure to dedicate a page to let them know what the technology resources were for students to access outside of school. Along with a page that outlined our rewards for positive decision making and behavior. Full confession, I think my students accessed the page more than their parents. In all honesty, we accessed it as a class daily for them to be able to do different tasks and assignments, so I am not surprised they were my frequent site viewers.

NEWSLETTERS (ELECTRONIC & PAPER FORM)

I would send newsletters occasionally throughout the year. The goal behind the newsletter would be to keep parents up to speed on what to expect in the coming weeks or months. In these newsletters, I would share positives, upcoming events, milestones reached, and where we would be headed next content-wise. This would also be another opportunity for me to re-direct them back to the webpage and remind them of my contact information.

CLASS DOJO

There are a lot of apps out there that you can use to connect with parents. I used Class Dojo to reach out to parents without having to exchange my personal info. This app also allowed me to give real-time feedback to parents throughout the day. With Class Dojo, I could create categories and assign positive or negative points to let parents know when students were displaying certain behaviors. Parents could also message me if they had questions over why their students were earning or losing points. Along with that, Class Dojo gave me a chance to send important information or reminders in case students forgot when they got home. It helped me reach far more parents than email since the app was right on their phone and they could get instant notifications.

Positive Contacts

I can't stress enough how important it is to make a positive contact home within those first couple of weeks of school. I hold to this because it can set the tone of how a student will do the remainder of the year. There have been plenty of students who came into my classroom saying how they were the "bad kid" years prior and did a complete flip because I pulled out the positives vs negatives early on. Even before contacting the parents, I would make sure to catch students doing great things and let them know days before contacting parents. The outcome would usually be that student beaming from the positive praise and each day they'd continue to build on all of the good things I had already pointed out to them.

Student Accountability

Along with the positive contact, the accountability contact is just as important. Yes, it is nice to see the positives in students and share that with everyone. However, make sure the student is getting accurate praise for what they are truly doing. There are times when you must address things with students. I found that addressing those issues with students directly helped them to reflect on their behavior. I would make time for a student to sit down with me and think about their action vs the expectation. Once a student could identify to me what the expected behavior was, we would make a plan to ensure the negative behavior didn't happen again. I would always outline the next steps if behavior didn't change. One of the last actions within the classroom would be a contact home which I would have students take ownership of.

Partnership Contact Home (last result)

If the student accountability session did not work, I would move into a parent contact. Keep in mind, this would normally come after many chances of having the student talk with me and make a plan. The parent contact meant the student would call and explain to parents what had been happening. Or I'd have them write a note that had to be signed by an adult by the next morning or we would call together on the student's time (i.e a few minutes into their favorite special, library checkout etc). They would explain how many times we had addressed the issue and why it was continuing. From there we would come up with a plan that included a parent or guardian's voice. I would then make sure I checked in within a set timeframe to let the parent know how things were going.

Summary

Parents play a critical and vital role when it comes to a student's learning success. Growing up, I never wanted my school to contact home. The contact home always came with a negative tone. As an educator, I wanted to change that narrative. I did not want my contact home to always be about bad behavior. So, using all these different strategies helped me to connect with the home as best I could. Full confession, you may do all these things and not hear from a student's parent once throughout the year or get a response. I learned over time that is okay! As long as you are being consistent in your communication and practice you are serving your purpose.

As an educator, I had to think of my parents as a partner and not the disciplinarian to make their child behave at school. I also had to think about what my parent's experiences in school were and many had the same mindset as me. I didn't want to overload them with every minor issue and risk them shutting me out or just being overly concerned each day. I wanted to find that balance between informing parents vs mandating they step in. I also wanted to have a relationship with my students that showed them that their decision-making is what drives their outcomes. By relying too heavily on parents to step in and solve their student's problems it takes accountability off the plate of the student. My goal was to help students understand the positives and negatives and by the time we got to parents, it was clear that we needed outside help to get them back on track.

Did I have parents who contacted me more than others or wanted information more frequently than others? Yes. I made sure that just like with my students, I accommodated those needs if I knew about this preference. The reality is most parents have many other priorities throughout their day. Calling them every single day to address an issue is an inconvenience. Especially if there is a way you can set up your management plan or work with the student to minimize the issue. Collaboration, awareness, and partnership is the best way I navigated parent relationships as a new teacher. Just like your students, no two years are the same. The same holds for the partnership you will have with parents.

Chapter 3
#Selfies: The True Relationship Builder

Be True to You!

One thing I learned about myself early on in teaching is that I would never be that teacher that just magically starts doing things because it's the new viral trend on YouTube. Which meant you'd never catch me randomly dancing. Full confession, I can keep a beat, but a whole dance routine? Pushing it! No random raps or handshakes were happening in the Queendom from me, but these were all things my class had complete freedom to do and express through their learning. What I did do was find something I enjoyed and overly exaggerated it to connect with my students. The thing that worked for me were selfies (Pre-Covid 19 of course). In my very first year of teaching, I found myself taking pictures of everything and my students would always hop in the shot or pose when they would see me capturing something. I knew at the end of the year I would make some sort of slide show, so my goal was to have enough footage to make a good memory keepsake for my students. The pictures also made it easy for me to share what we were doing on my class webpage vs writing out a newsletter all the time. After the first year, I thought about how I could use pictures to build relationships and brag on and show off my students. I would often tell them that I knew coming into the year that I had the best class in the building and wanted to brag on them and show them off.

So, my second year and beyond I would start the year with an "I Believe In My Selfie" activity. Students would write goals and positive affirmations about what they would commit to doing throughout the year. I would do the activity myself to model the expectation and the final product would be displayed in the hallway. I would of course take my selfie in front of the class while explaining the assignment and then give students the option to take a selfie with me or one by themselves. I made sure to complete this activity within the first week of school. As with any classroom, I wanted to be mindful of my shy students or those students who still needed more time to get to know me. I did not want to force them to be in a picture with me. However, I often found that most students would want to take their selfies with me which was an added perk to kick the year off. The final caveat was that I would give them each a crown. The crown would be earned by them completing the first draft of their selfie affirmation then writing the final form in cursive after I had checked it. My spiel to them was after they earned their crown it would be up to them to be able to keep it based on how they chose to complete their year.

During work time, I would call back students who were finished up with their final draft to receive their crown and choose how they wanted to take their picture. Some students did not feel comfortable doing their picture with the whole class in the room, so I'd allow them to take a quick one on our way to specials, at recess, at the end of the day, or whatever made them feel comfortable. Options are a must in any classroom since you have so many unique individuals. The final execution of the task was printing their pictures and getting their pages hung up in the hallway. I can still feel the excitement of when they'd show up and see all of our class selfies in the hallway and they'd tell me how their friends in other classes would say how cool it was. From that moment on pictures were always our thing. What I found amazing is there were even students who would start the year saying they hated pictures and I would allow them to hide or not be in the pictures if they chose; and as the year crept on, I would see them actively joining in and smiling when it came time to capture different things happening in our room.

Yes, selfies, crowns, calling them my Prince & Princesses, and giving them nicknames were MY thing as a teacher. Students knew what to expect, they knew what activities I would more than likely get my camera, crowns, or anything royalty-related out for. Their nicknames would come about a month or two into the year. By this time, I would have had enough lunches, hung out at recess with them, and just had opportunities to chat to give them the perfect nickname (which usually was a twist on their original first or last name). They would love the names that I would give them and often call me out if I went a long time without using them. I would use these incentives up until our end-of-year red carpet party where we would have our crowns, a selfie booth, and celebrate all our success from the year. Although selfies were the main thing that worked for me starting out, I had to have way more in my arsenal than that to continue building relationships with students. Below I will list some examples of other things I did that naturally helped me bond with my students. The bright side is a lot of these ideas I was able to gather from my students based on their feedback so it did not take much thinking for me to find things they would like.

- Using their letters from the start of the year to incorporate playing music during independent work time. I would get their favorite songs and create a class list with Kids Bop versions of the songs they requested.
- Collectively getting whole class ideas of what types of rewards and prizes they would like if we hit certain reward targets (i.e. if we earned 15 class paws we would have technology day etc.).
- Continuing with lunch bunches
- Walking the trail during recess with the class
- Interacting in activities at recess (shout of four square and basketball games! Yes, sometimes I'd

have a dress and my J's on playing basketball at recess 😊)

- If students wrote me a letter, taking the time to write them back and respond to whatever it is they had communicated to me.
- Giving out random certificates to place a spotlight on behaviors that students may randomly start slipping in to help reinforce the expectation. For example, if we had a long week of students not following line expectations, I would randomly give certificates to 3 or 4 kids who had been leaders in that area and invite them to lunch instead of calling the whole class out on what was going wrong. Change the narrative!
- Sending home positive notes for each student at some point during the first part of the year.
- Giving students a chance to troubleshoot any issues first before telling them what to do. For example, if a student is doing more talking than working. Asking the student what is causing them to lose focus. If they said it is who they were sitting by, then I would let them know I would change their seat the next chance I got, but if the behavior continued, we would have to discuss further why it keeps happening.
- Trusting students to work out a plan with me first before calling parents about negative behavior was a huge trust builder for me. Most times, the independent conversation with me and a plan helped that student correct the behavior. I usually never would have to take the final step of following up with home.

These are again, just a few examples, not an all-inclusive list. I often found that I needed an arsenal full of things to meet the needs of each student and no one-two things always worked the same. Some things would work at the beginning of the year and would not be effective by winter break or springtime. So, I found it was a constant rotation of strategies to keep students with me throughout the year. My biggest piece of advice would be to find what works for you and continue to refine and run with it. It may not hook every single student, but there will be elements that you will find every student enjoys.

So, go ahead be YOU and let everything else fall into place! Trust me, your students will know who is not being authentic and have no shame bringing it up to you over a chocolate milk and the latest school lunch entrée.

Chapter 4
Consistency Is Key

Behavior Management: Proactive vs Reactive

Negative behavior. We eat, sleep, dread and fear it as a new teacher. One thing my teacher prep program did prepare me for was to expect negative behavior. I had pages full of strategies that I had no clue on what the outcome would be when the time came to use them. As years went on, I would see from in-person field experiences that this negative behavior took on many forms with the biggest shape being disrespect at times. I wanted to teach, but I dreaded going into a role that presented constant disrespect each day. While I feel like I found my voice to lead a class by the end of my field experiences, I still was the quiet soft-spoken woman who battled with how serious students would take me. Luckily, taking a break and entering the education world after becoming a parent granted me balance. I found that I could still be who I was and instill the same qualities in my students that I had for my own daughter. That is when the light bulb went off, that yes, I needed to be a teacher with planned consequences, and I needed to be consistent when those times arose. I wanted my classroom management plan to operate from a pro-active lens vs being strictly reactive. I also wanted to be the teacher that attached consequences to the behavior, not because there were learning gaps.

Full confession, I had a middle school teacher that I did not care for. I felt he had great stories, he had a strong firm approach, but he lacked empathy when it came to learning. As one of his students, you were liable to receive the same consequence for doing badly on a test just as much as a kid who had no shame cursing him out to his face. I still remember doing bad on a random science test one time and saw the wrath other kids had repeatedly faced in all other subject areas they may have struggled with. He slammed the door and repeatedly yelled the question and then called names out loud for people to give him the answer. Which it was clear that the people in the room did not know, remember, or just was not prepared for the test so trying to force an answer out of us was not the solution. I remember sitting there thinking how awful of a teacher he was that his first solution was to scream at kids about not doing well on one test vs trying to find the solution on why most of his class did not do well. I never wanted to be that teacher and from day one decided that I would never be a teacher that yelled. Which was a trait that helped me with being proactive vs reactive. Was there a way to be firm with expectations and still come across as nurturing? Yes, I fully believed there was, and I hope that is how I came across to my students.

The thing with behavior management is you can never be prepared for it. Of course, there may be students that could display patterns or predictability of when certain triggers may result in certain responses, but there is not a set way to determine who is going to have a bad day vs who will not.

As a new teacher that is the balance, you want to ensure learning can happen. I remember being a new teacher and it never failed that every year the year would start rockier than I always expected. One school I was at, I remember having the first day planned, the morning went amazing, and I was hit in the face with the afternoon chaos. I found that once specials, lunch & recess hit, the afternoon would turn brutal. I realized this was happening because of student's comfort level shifting after the morning, past confrontations being brought to the front at recess, and some students even settling on the fact that the new year was going to be a continuation of the reputation they had gained the past school year. I had two choices at that moment, cave and let them go about as normal which I knew would get increasingly worse throughout the year or come up with a plan.

Full confession, that day when I left, I had no plan. All I knew was that I did not want to go back the next day after seeing how the kids had treated each other and disrespected our learning space with arguing, being loud, and outright no self-control. Every scenario played in my head about how to leave the position. After sitting in my car for what seemed like forever (literally probably 10 minutes in shock) I decided my best bet would be to get through the year and leave that building as soon as the year was over. It was a feeling of defeat that lingered with me all that evening into the night. I could not fathom how to handle another afternoon let alone a day of what I had seen. It was not until later that night where I kicked it into gear and decided that my year was not going to be defined by having one bad afternoon on my first day in a brand-new school with kids I had never built a relationship with before. So, I came up with a completely new plan of how I would manage that group and even those individual 4 students who seemed to be outliers during all the disruption I had witnessed the day before. So, what happened?

I stuck with my morning plan, same expectations in place. My focus was to stick with the positive and keep the positivity in those moments where they had displayed it and not ruin it with a "lecture". Sure enough, the morning went as expected, we had a great community circle. We got a chance to talk about some more expectations and even practice tightening up the things we had done well the day before. We were all in good spirits doing what needed to be done. During work time I had started having "student meetings" where I would call them back to the table to have them read to me and just get to know them more. I made sure I got a meeting in with those 4 students who were apart of the chaos from the day before. That is when I learned who had "plans" from last year based on how they described past accommodations. What they liked and hated about school. Along with who they felt they had issues with inside of our class and one thing that they thought would benefit them to be successful.

One student requested to have their desk in a certain part of the room away from specific students, another said to switch a line spot, one asked to take a break occasionally, and the other one asked to sit at the back table for the rest of the week during independent time. Done! All things I could manage and commitments I could make to show them I valued their feedback so that when the time came for me to give them constructive feedback hopefully, they would take it. Of course, we still had the afternoon to look forward to.

Like clockwork, the same issue as the day before. Afternoon starts, the same type of loud entering, kids arguing back and forth over a game in specials. One kid completely in need of a cool down just banging on the desk with his hands. Some students with their heads down, one covering their ears. In my mind, I was thinking, "Here we were again, day 2".

The only difference was today there was not an early out and we had way more time before leaving that could not be fluffed through to keep the peace. So, I needed to jump into action. I called everyone to the carpet and stood there silent for at least 5 minutes just looking at them. Inside I was having an explosive meltdown, but my physical demeanor exuded calm, firmness, disappointment, and leadership. That stance gradually brought all the chatter, side comments, mini arguments/outbursts to a stop. Once it was all eyes staring back at me in confusion, I heard my voice. Again, no yelling necessary, just a firm, assertive tone. The first thing that came out was,

"THIS IS COMPLETED UNACCEPTABLE! AND MOST DEFINITELY THE HIGHEST FORM OF DISRESPECT I HAVE EVER SEEN OUT OF A CLASS! WHAT IS DISAPPOINTING IS THAT THIS IS DAY 2 OF THE SAME THING HAPPENING IN THE AFTERNOON AND SOME PEOPLE THINK THIS IS OKAY WHEN IT IS NOT. WE HAVE HAD THESE GREAT TALKS IN THE MORNING AND MADE AGREEMENTS ON WHAT YOU THINK RESPECT LOOKS LIKE FROM ME AS YOUR TEACHER AND FROM YOUR PEERS IN THE CLASSROOM AND WE ARE NOT SHOWING ANY OF THAT RIGHT NOW"

I followed this with another 1-minute silent pause to give them time to reflect. After some reflective time, my follow-up question was, "Who can tell me what unexpected behaviors have been happening since we stepped foot back into the classroom?" At that point, hands started raising. One thing I had to do early on was teach my class how to have an open reflective conversation as a group without triggering those escalated students. I taught them that when we were addressing unexpected behaviors as a whole class that we would call out the behavior not the specific name of the students doing it. Instead of saying, "because _______ is arguing is _______", students would say, "the unexpected behavior is students are arguing back and forth". Then I would type their responses on the smartboard as they were calling them out. Once finished, I would have them sit silently and read over the responses.

Next, this step always was the turning point for me. Accountability. My next step would be to have students pinpoint what part they played in the situation we were addressing. This meant them going back to their seats, taking out a sheet of paper, and telling me their role in this specific incident. I would always tell them, "if you were doing the expected behaviors then please tell me that". By having students go back to their seat and write in silence it would help some students calm down and give me a chance to get to the students who were heavily escalated. The highly agitated students usually were not ready to write anyway. It would allow me to offer them a think station break and let them write in the break space or let them just quietly talk with me about what was going on. In this situation, I did have one student storm out of the room, and I allowed that situation to happen and moved on with my class (I'll circle back to that student later). Once all students were done writing and brought me their notes, I would give them a different independent task and read their feedback in real-time during that moment. Yes, it went off schedule from my original plan, but taking this time in the beginning to correct these behaviors had great lasting results throughout the remainder of the year.

For this situation, I read all notes in real-time and put them in piles, expected behaviors vs unexpected behaviors. I brought the class back to the carpet and without using names gave them the data based on their reflections. I had let them know that 9 people felt they were showing expected behaviors while 11 said they contributed to the disruption. I always thanked them for being reflective whether it was good or bad. Once they heard the data, we would come up with a plan as a class. For this class, they felt that coming in the room with the lights off and being given 5 minutes to calm down would help them fully transition. So, again it's a partnership, I told them I could do that with the trust that I would not see anything like I had seen the past two days. So, while I was reactive to what I saw the first day, I used the next day when the situation presented itself to get proactive with what would happen moving forward if this happened again. I agreed to allow 5 minutes as a cool down and that also had to be a time for students still struggling to connect with me if 5 minutes was not going to help. I also let them know that I would be keeping their letters. Moving forward, if those same unexpected behaviors are displayed our next step would be me and them discussing the behavior with a parent or guardian.

I always allowed my students to call out unexpected behavior, create a plan with me first before bringing parents into it. I feel that this strengthened my trust with a lot of students because many went on and never had to go to that next step of reaching out to parents with me. As for the student that walked out, the expectation did not change for him. I waited until the next day when he was in a better mindset and we talked about what the expected behaviors were. He completed the same letter task as the rest of the class and was brought up to speed on what our class plan was moving forward. While it took him longer to complete his accountability task, it got done and it made a whole class incident go from being a pattern to be an one-off situation. I found my management style always consisted of calling out the unexpected behavior (if it was most of the class then the whole group, if specific incidences then just that student), having students reflect for accountability, putting in place a natural consequence, and proactively setting the scene of next steps if the behaviors continued.

Principal's Office

I was not a "go to the principal's office" teacher. I wanted the office to be the last resort because ultimately those students would be coming back to my classroom every day. I did not want their fear to be having an office visit every single day. While it took a lot of balancing, patience, letting things go, and circling back, I found a way to make it work. By doing this, it also helped my students see that I was not going to let them run from the problem and that they would be held accountable for what they needed to do. For some students, their goal is to escape even if it means going to the principal's office. Escaping was often the easy route when they would want to skip out on an unpreferred task. By finding different ways to keep them in the classroom, it allowed me the opportunity to keep them in the room. They would be listening to the skill being learned even if that meant they would have to complete the actual task later when they were calm and able to focus.

Now do not get me wrong, I am not saying that I never used the principal's office because I did. However, in those instances it was usually when all other tier 1 classroom strategies had been exhausted, the unexpected behavior had been addressed multiple times with parents now in the loop or to adhere to special tier intervention or IEP plans. Usually, if it did get this far, I would have already been in contact with the building student support specialist and principal about the behavior. I did not feel comfortable just leaving them to figure it out, my emails and communication would often detail what had happened, what had been tried, and even a solution to combat the behavior. Contact and consistency are vital in dealing with any student. I had some students who just needed to see that I would follow through with the consequences if they kept repeating unexpected behaviors. Thankfully, I had administrators that showed full support when I needed them to step in.

Proactive? Tell Me More

While I can't say there is a solid airtight classroom management plan, I have found there are ways to plan for how you will respond and address issues. As I've stated, I'd always address the concern with my students first, give them a chance to explain why, and come up with a plan to prevent the same unexpected behaviors from happening. In our conversations, I would always ask, "How would your parent (or guardian) feel if they hear about how you acted today?". This would help me understand if this was a behavior allowed at home or if they were acting out at school for peers. Below, I will list some of the things I put in place to help combat behavior before it became a "big thing". These were behaviors that students would tell me about themselves or things I may have noticed by just interacting with the students. I also considered if the behaviors were things being identified by specials teachers or support staff. I would normally set something in place so that my students would not carry those actions over into our learning environment. Full confession, I am not saying these are the perfect solutions, but I found these were actions differentiated enough that they helped me keep trust with my students and hold them to a high standard of making good decisions at school.

Unexpected behavior	How I addressed it Prior to Office Assistance?
Taking a large amount of time to transition (whole class or independently)	*Put marks on the board indicating how many minutes of learning time they had used that I would get back from a preferred activity of their choice. If individual and a repeated pattern, I'd keep a tally on a note pad to share with the student and they would give that time back to me during one of their preferred tasks.*

Verbal disrespect	*On student's time have them complete a "Respect Note" to hold them accountable for the action. After we had conferenced on the behavior, they'd then write a letter reflecting on the unexpected behavior. Give them a choice to apologize verbally or in writing. Made students aware if it happened again, we'd call home to share that this behavior continues to happen and come up with a plan for it to stop with parents.*
Student using curse words when mad at peers	*Met with that student, found out it was okay for them to speak this way at home. Explained the difference between home and school. We came up with a plan that the student could use a journal if they were triggered enough to want to use this language. What they put in the journal would be confidential and a way for them to decompress ONLY if they decided to walk away from the situation and get the journal vs saying what they were feeling to that person's face directly.*

Student Prefers to Draw instead of engaging in assigned classwork	*Gave student an "If, then" option. I would say, "If you complete the current task, then you can have the rest of the time to draw. That meant completing the task at grade level expectation, not just rushing through to say the task was finished.*

I could go on and on about classroom management. It is the foundation to be able to get into teaching students the skills they need to learn. Every year I focused a little more on putting relationships, routines, and procedures into place first and the rest fell into place shortly after. I also had to learn when it was necessary to speak more firmly versus leaving it up to chance that a student would understand the seriousness of my request. I found management to be a fun area to focus on being a new teacher. I ended up getting creative with creating whole class and individual incentives that motivated students. Coming from corporate America, I realized how much I appreciated the small tangibles (i.e., gift cards, t-shirts, certificates, small tokens of appreciation left on my desk randomly).

I thought that if I found that motivating as an adult, I was sure kids would appreciate the same sentiments. I found that classroom management ended up being a strong area of mine, potentially because I overly stressed about it the most and wanted to be proactive.

However, it was an area that I found my groove in that worked well for me. I am fully aware that every student may not have liked my approach, but I can say they respected it. Which allowed me to have an environment that had more positive moments vs negative. As I reflect, I can say for certain that students knew what to expect coming into our room. Eventually, other building staff knew exactly what to expect walking into my classroom as well. It was going to always be a quiet place where people could be calm and work. We would do fun things and have fun experiences, but a heavy focus was always on safety and being calm. My students also knew that if they were having a bad day, something as simple as writing me a note or asking me to speak with them before making a big disruption would benefit our whole class. I do pride myself on the management that I was able to create as a new teacher based on trial and error. I think my approach helped me teach my students social skills and what it meant to be a leader and show good character.

As I reflect on the many strategies I used, I realize it did help keep my classroom calm and I was able to keep a lot of students in the classroom. This ultimately led me to be able to do what my job role entailed, which was to teach.

Chapter 5
Differentiation: What's the hype about?

Equity over Equality

Full confession, early on in my teacher prep program I often thought equal treatment of my students HAD to be the way. It was a mindset that I thought would help each student. To make learning fair for all my students I thought kids would get every skill! WRONG! Student teaching busted this myth, thankfully. It was not long before I realized that the one size fits all approach was not the way to go. It was not even a full week into my first year of teaching that I fully grasped for myself that each student needed me in their own way. Yes, during student teaching I was following another teacher's plan so the groups, one on ones, offering various ways to complete assignments did not sit with me until I had my very own classroom. Sure, I could plan out a lesson and teach it, but what I did next would be especially important in ensuring student success. I needed to find ways to tap into student's minds and see what they understood and be prepared to fill the gaps or extend their thinking to help them truly learn. I found that differentiation was not just for academics, but even social-emotional and behavioral aspects within the classroom.

I recall having to push myself to loosen the reigns and allow different things to happen in my class that may not have been happening in any other classroom in the building. While it might be comfortable to have students listen to you talk for 20-30 minutes then go back to their seats and do a worksheet; it is not an ideal way for students to learn. It took collecting data, reviewing data, and being committed to testing out changes for me to be comfortable with all of the differentiation I planned for my classroom.

The biggest "aha" for me was using my student's voices to drive what learning looked like in our classroom. I would often have them write what was going well, what they hated, and anything I could change. That student voice piece is huge if you really want to get into equity. It may come with tough responses, but if you learn to not take it personal and use that feedback to make changes, it will be worth it. Your students will also respect you more for being vulnerable and flexible to make change. I would let them know that I would not be mad about anything they said and would take their feedback into account. I would do this sporadically throughout the year. My goal was to hear their voice and use it for change in our learning environment. I think of all the surveys teachers take and most times I wondered what would come of it. Many times, there was not much follow-up. I wanted to make sure my students knew that I appreciated them taking the time to let me know how they were feeling and enacted change immediately.

Differentiation is more than just making small groups. It is getting to the core of what drives students to be motivated, independent learners that can advocate for themselves vs shutting down. For the remainder of this chapter, I will break down some ways I incorporated differentiation based on various topic areas. If teachers genuinely want to ensure equity, it has to be done by doing what is right to the best of their ability for each student.

Whole Group:

With my whole class, differentiation happened in a lot of ways. I often found myself thinking of each type of learner I had while planning lessons. I made sure that the content I was teaching consisted of visual, auditory, and tangible practice of the skills. At any given point, you could walk into my room and see my students on the carpet, turning to talk to a partner, listening to a video or passage, or using manipulatives or a whiteboard to digest the learning I was providing. The style of learning is important along with the method in which the learning is delivered. I tried to stick to the 7-minute rule when it came to teaching. I believe it was a professional development meeting where I heard that students have an attention span of 7 minutes before they need to shift gears. I clung to that and it helped with managing behaviors as well. Often, I would start on the carpet. Explicitly explain what I would be teaching and what their learning target was by the end of the lesson. I would make sure to include some sort of opening hook to lock them into the lesson.

Throughout this time, I would teach based on their interest level. If I saw I was losing kids I would quickly switch gears and have them do something different that incorporated movement to bring their attention back. That movement could be standing and finding a partner to repeat what I just said, turning and talking to a partner about an answer, thinking about a question they had over the content and sharing it with a small group, or just stopping and taking a mental pause. This helped my learners who needed to have the content chunked out and those who needed to verbalize what I was saying before they could fully process the skill. My differentiation for the whole group also meant checking in with students to make sure I was not zipping through the lesson too fast. I would often do a quick thumbs-up, thumbs to side, or thumbs-down check-in. I would front load that our learning space was just that, a learning space at the beginning of the year to help students understand it was okay to share if they were struggling with something. I reiterated to them that it was okay to make mistakes.

Aside from academics, differentiation at the classroom management level looked just as diversified. I soon learned that there were times my whole class needed a 5-minute desk rest break after certain subjects to release and move forward. It also meant I would play music at a low level during the independent work time, let students sit in the hall or other places in the room if it was going to help their mood or learning.

Differentiation also presented itself in my routines and procedures. Yes, we all had a line procedure. However, how that looked varied from other rooms in the building. I remember having a plan in place where one student lined up last because it worked out best for them to wait until the rest of the class was in line showing the expectation. This student would often be triggered if they were in line doing their job and the whole class would have to go back to their seats to practice. Since this student had proved to me countlessly that they could show the line expectation each time, I trusted them in allowing that change. This was a low-level change that greatly enhanced the success of following these procedures by working with my students.

Differentiation also meant catering to the preferences of how my students wanted to be rewarded. I had a variety of positive acknowledgments available that I rotated through throughout the year. I used handwritten certificates, my Kudos Prize box, saving the book order points to give to students, stickers, positive emails/calls or notes, pictures, crowns, school tickets, class points, leadership challenges, and many other things that I did not hesitate to throw out there if it meant reaching a student at their level.

Small Groups

I went into teaching thinking yes; I'll have these fancy small groups and that I would meet with kids each day etc. I soon found that while small groups were great for learning, I needed to differentiate how that looked on any given day or week. That meant, using the data to group my kids and picking activities that tapped into their level. Walking into my room during small group time meant students would be on technology, working independently, in some sort of collaboration group, or meeting with me.

The other duties unassigned were me spending many hours outside of school finding good learning skill videos and games that matched the skill vs letting students have a free for all pick. Differentiation also meant prioritizing what groups needed to see me when. If that meant meeting with group 1 at the beginning and end of rotations, then so be it. If it meant I had a group that could independently complete a project without much guidance from me- great! In some groups, I would need to use a menu of multiple strategies to help them grasp the understanding of a skill while other groups may be able to use one solid strategy to show their comprehension. It was a balancing act where I let my student data and feedback drive what I offered during those learning times.

INDEPENDENT

Independent differentiation was by far my best type of differentiation. It meant I could build a relationship with a student and find out what worked for them. This type of differentiation was critical for me to be able to adjust at the perfect time to ensure a student would not shut down. My goal was to always keep students open to whatever it was we were learning even if they hated it. For example, I had one student who did not like writing. He felt he was not good at it and early on would find ways to avoid tasks no matter what varied options I gave for completion. By having a one on one with the student I found that he loved to draw. He would much rather draw his thoughts vs write. We agreed that if he completed the writing task, he could make illustrations for the remainder of the time. However, he knew it needed to be grade-level appropriate and not a rush job. My goal was to always work with the student to get them to practice or show the skill without removing the overall expectation.

I found that as time went on, he was writing way more before getting to his art and grew to be an even better writer by the end of the year. He would often write stories for me and put the pages together as a book with drawings using outside of school time as well.

For my students who did not like math and struggled independently, I set up a system where I would give them the answers to the problems and their job was to show the steps or be able to ask me a specific question on where their thinking error began. This was a game-changer because often students just sit during an independent work time and do not complete a thing. Having the answers gave students that boost to start on something. I often did not realize how many different plans I had with students until the end of the year when we would reflect on their growth and what they felt contributed to it. While it may have created extra mental and physical work for me at times to manage, the benefit far outweighed the time spent.

GRADING

Grading differentiation was the last area I focused on that I wish I would have noticed first. A lot of students have a bad picture of school often based on prior-year grades and what they perceive their learning strengths or abilities to be. I later learned that what I viewed as an assessment was not an inclusive look at what my students knew. I remember growing up being a horrible test taker in subjects I did not prefer. However, I achieved in the other areas that I did like and felt confident in. Knowing that, I wanted to be more mindful of the various ways students could show me their learning outside of tests.

In my classroom, you would find students doing more than paper pencil worksheets or tests. I would often put them in groups to work and the added layer of assessment would come from their reflection. I would often have each student assess their contribution to the group. Thankfully, I had students who were honest with themselves on what they felt they did well and how they could have improved. I also allowed students to be involved in challenges against themselves. For instance, in my final year, I did a "Beat the Bitmoji" reading challenge. I took student's reading scores from the prior year and conferenced with them independently to set a goal on where they felt they could improve by different checkpoints throughout the year.

Students would have weeks to use any free time to practice for that challenge and strengthen the skill and their "assessment" would be reading with me on the checkpoint date privately. There were times students would zoom past their goal and there were students who I knew were working hard and fell short, but that was ok. I would ask them what they felt would help. Some asked to read the next day because they were not feeling well, tired, etc. and I allowed it. Many would meet that goal the next day just like they had predicted. Others would still fall short, but would have had the opportunity to see from me that failure is not an option and I was open to helping them as much as I could.

I hated giving students tests because many factors could play into why they did or did not do well. I recall having a student who had been on a list for intervention before coming to me. After a few weeks, I realized she was one of the highest students in my class in that subject area. So, being thoroughly confused, I would watch her, look over her work and tests to figure out what the deal was. I soon learned that her limitation was that she just went slower than other kids. She essentially just needed more time. She was thorough and wanted to read and re-read the questions along with writing clear answers. I pulled her to the side and asked if she just needed more time. She said yes that her biggest issue was that she did not write fast enough to finish on time. I worked out a plan with her that she could have extra time to finish the test the next day since her answers were right. She was just losing points by not finishing and that changed everything for her. She became one of my top peer leaders to work with other students and the test anxiety she had starting during the year had reduced greatly. So, with grading, there are a lot of different accommodations you can make to help students display mastery in multiple ways. Our kids are so creative and a paper-pencil test is not the most accurate view of all they can do. Try to work with them!

Differentiation is that thing that is near and dear to my heart because I always thought back on my own education and what worked. There were subjects I excelled in and some that took a little more thinking and effort out of me. Had my teachers not worked with me in unique ways I would not have been so successful. Taking some time to think outside of the box is not a bad thing, it is a necessary priority that will only benefit you and your students across the board.

Chapter 6

The Student Becomes the Teacher

Ode to My Favorite Educator

As I think back to making the decision to go into teaching, I always remembered what brought me to the classroom. Sure, many things deterred me from joining the profession at first. There were so many myths that I soon realized were from people who did not know how the education field truly operated. However, one minor experience to some is what fueled me to leap. The elementary years go by so fast and often get overlooked as the key game-changers in the lives of those little people. For me, it was all that I knew. It was the elementary years that showed me that adults not related to me could genuinely care about my success. Those were not pretty times for my family which made those adult relationships even more appreciated by me.

I remember having a parent who was incarcerated during a part of my elementary years. My school counselor would offer and take us up to the prison for visits. No strings attached just being a good genuine person. When I found people like that I went above and beyond to not let them down. Was I a perfect angel? No! A good student overall? Yes. However, to these individuals that went above and beyond, I never wanted them to see a version of me lower than the expectation they had set.

I soon found that with my students. We had such a great relationship and bond that I would have students doing great for me in my room. Then they would get to other areas and not do so well. For a long time, I could not figure out why. I often thought it was my place to step in and try to fix those issues between my students and other adults then the light bulb went off that I couldn't fix those relationships with other adults. I did the same thing growing up. The major source of why I made the decisions I made with certain teachers or staff was based purely on our relationship and their bond with me. If they looked at me as a test score or point on a graph, they did not get the best version of me and I honestly did not care.

I had an amazing 4th & 5th grade teacher. She instilled a level of motivation and determination in me that no other educator had ever been able to accomplish.

Yes, we did fun things all the time. She made learning fun, but I also knew that she could take those fun things away at any moment and I would still respect her the same. I never wanted to let her down because she had built up my confidence level in a way that I just knew I could do anything I put my mind to. I had to remind myself of this during my time in the classroom. A lot of my students never wanted to let me down. So, they would always do their personal best for me. I found this true whether I was giving prizes, not giving prizes, waiting for our class to earn a reward, or repeatedly practicing procedures while they had angry looks on their faces. While they may have been mad because I was holding them to expectations or putting a pause on things, I didn't feel like their respect lessened during these moments. They always followed through to show me they respected me enough to show me the good version of them. It was the same thing I did as a student.

I realized my 4th and 5th grade years mirrored the type of teacher I became in my classroom. Students that were not in my class either expressed interest in wanting to be in my room or outright hated what my class got to do--no in-between LOL! "It's not fair"! is what a lot of my students would hear. I completely understood those students because outside of those two years I experienced during my elementary years; I did not enjoy school much after that. It always seemed like other classes got to do fun things. I would always tell my class, "We can't control what their teachers do in their rooms, we can only control what happens in here. I base what happens in here on your actions and decisions". I never wanted my students to feel bad for being rewarded because if you know me, you know they earned it. I did not just give out rewards to bribe my students. It was only meant to celebrate successes that were happening in the classroom. I communicated that to my students in the beginning. One of my spiels is always that in life you often do not get the credit you deserve, but that one moment you do it feels amazing. I would set them up to know that we had all of these positive consequences in place, but I would decide based on their decision-making when to use them. It would be random so that kids would be doing more of the right thing all the time vs at the moment for praise. There were times I would go weeks without handing out a prize or we would have met our ticket goal and had not done a celebration yet. However, it did not change my student's behavior and respect towards me. But when we celebrated, it was pure royalty. Yes, I'm extra and go all out to celebrate the positive!

I often think about the $700 tree I bought in 4th grade with all my scholar dollars. My teacher had been passing out fake school money all year that she called Scholar Dollars. Out of all the money I had earned I got a tree LOL! My classmates did not understand it in the least bit, but this tree was EVERYTHING! It had different treats tied to the branches and was decorated so nicely. Plus, the tree itself was something I could give to my mom. So yes, I spent every dollar to get it. I will never forget the feeling of buying this tree and this was the feeling I wanted my students to experience multiple times throughout our year together. Little did Mrs. B.

know; she was showing me early on how to celebrate myself. I enjoyed her class because she made it fun but connected so much of it to reality. I remember getting the class job of being the banker and I got to use her fancy jeweled button calculator in that role. This is where I learned how to keep a financial record. I remember learning how to balance a checkbook and even understanding how to save money for something bigger from her.

It came full circle later in my own classroom. In my room fun mixed with reality looked like, inviting a diverse range of guests in to share skills, information, and have students see people of color in positions they often did not associate them with having. I also used scholar dollars at the start of each year, and it was up to the class to keep them. If I remember correctly, two of my classes made it to the mid-year holiday auction where community members would donate toys and activities that students could buy and take home before the holiday break. The auction was the same experience my 4th and 5th grade teacher had given me. I had reading challenges where I was able to get grade-level books for cheap from local bookstores to give to students to keep them reading outside of the school year. A huge event was bringing in local business owners and one owner holding mock interviews with my students to help them prepare for the job after we had completed resumes as a writing unit. A sentimental moment was if I ever received flowers at school, I would give them all a rose to take home and give to an important person in their lives. We talked often about the importance of thanking people who play a valuable role in our lives. When I graduated with my Master of Science degree in Educational Leadership, guess what, they too celebrated with me by attending my classroom graduation party. A moment I will never forget is one year having a class where students said they had never had hot cocoa and cookies. So, we set a high-ticket goal, achieved it and they experienced their first hot cocoa, animal crackers, and movie time with me. Thankfully, this was before all of the Blue Zone healthy snack rules 😊. My favorite by far has always been the end-of-year Red Carpet party. This was to instill in students when it was appropriate to go all out and get dressed up to participate in a fancy event. To let them know when they are getting celebrated it is okay to look their best. At that party, I would hand out rewards, allow leaders to decorate the room the night before, we would have snacks, a photo booth, and parents could come. The awards they would receive were based on their peers' feedback along with mine. This one event taught so many life skills. What a perfect way to close off the year!

As a teacher, I know the focus is on content and skills, but the social aspect of what we do has to be present. We are teaching our kids how to be productive citizens. We owe them experiences that prepare them for what to expect in the real world and teaches them how to celebrate their wins. If Mrs. B taught me anything, it was that there is a way to navigate life and make it fun. I hope each of my students felt that way leaving my room. I hope all of them encounter moments in their personal lives that connect to a moment in our school year and can say I helped prepare them for that. The unassigned duties, the duties others might consider time-consuming or doing too much are always worth it. Thank you, Mrs. B, for showing me all of this. As your student, I learned so much about how to be an influential teacher versus just an academic one.

Chapter 7
Check Your Work-Life Balance!

Is there such a thing as work-life balance in teaching? Yes! Did I have it in my first year of teaching? No! That first year was a learning curve for me for sure. I will admit, I dedicated a lot of time to making things and wanting to make everything look just right. I also wanted to make each lesson my own and put some personality into the content. In my first year, I had a great team that provided me with everything I needed from a scheduling and content standpoint. However, understanding how to figure out the timing and pacing of lessons and units was the thing I had to figure out on my own. I consider the first year like flying a plane for the first time with an emphasis on just being able to arrive at the destination safely as the main goal. My safe destination was the end of the school year with students showing growth in some way shape or form. I did not have it all together. I often did not realize all of my official duties until someone told me where to be and when, but I knew I could not stop the flight. We might have had some turbulence, but I refused to give up on my students and teaching role.

In my first year, I had no balance. Work merged into my home life often. I thankfully had waited to go into teaching until my child was school-aged, so that helped me to do some extra things when she was in bed. I found myself doing a lot of grading at home, printing, laminating, planning my daily lessons, trying to respond to every email, signing up for things within my building to feel like I was contributing, and figuring out ways to make learning fun. Having had come out of a long-term substitute position, I had some knowledge about certain things, but it was surface level through another teacher's lens. During the long-term substitute role, those plans were completely laid out for that time vs my first year of teaching being all on me to create. I'd often set up behavior systems and games along with making all of the charts and posters I needed to accompany my lesson. It was A LOT, to say the least. I expected it though, which is where my reality came in. I knew it wouldn't be forever based on all of the helpful advice from the experienced teachers I worked with, but for that first year, I needed to grind through it. When the second year came, the game changed!

Teacher Mode-The Sequels

That second year changed my life. Not only was I going into it with tools I had spent time on during my first year that could be utilized; but I also had insight into what I was teaching. Sticking with the same grade level brought comfort from a curriculum standpoint. Along with just knowing the ropes of a school building and typical year brought more confidence. Now I just needed to execute what I knew from the standards side. My focus to make learning even more engaging with opportunities for students to practice and master the skills. Starting the second year and beyond I stepped up in all the ways I could to utilize my time during the day to complete things and not bring as much stuff home as the first year. It was a big improvement from my first year. I am going to go into more detail on which parts of my day or week specifically helped me get my life balance back.

Weekly Planning

I began by doing a simple one-page electronic planning agenda for the week. Like literally a 5 by however many slots my schedule had each day. It was a table in MS Word. To complete my weekly schedule, I would block off time on early Sunday mornings to do it. My firm time dedication was to be done by 10 am since usually I would always be up between 8:30-9:00am. Whatever I didn't get done by 10 am would be finished in my prep time on Monday. Usually, I'd at least have the first half of the week done within that 1-2 hours of planning, so it worked out this way. This plan would include my daily schedule and a breakdown of what the topic or skill was for each day. I'd also have a spot at the bottom of the page with reminders for the week (i.e IEP Mtgs, coaching/PLC meetings, committee meetings, library checkout days, lab days, upcoming events, celebrations, parents to contact etc.). This schedule worked wonders because I could share it with the support staff that was assisting in my room. It was also a quick way I could see what times were available if I did need to schedule something extra.

Coaching Meetings

Game changer! Some teachers do not prefer to use their prep for coaching meetings. I get it, if you plan day by day, your prep may be the only time you have to prepare things. However, I personally welcomed these meetings as I often found ways to reflect on my areas of growth and sync up everything in general. My coaching feedback would often fit my needs unless there was a building focus for those cycles. If I needed a look at how to tighten up a transition or execute a group project, those extra sets of eyes were huge in helping me see the things I could not see while teaching. Seek out and embrace the coaching and co-plan sessions if your building has this. Most times, if I needed a form or something my coach would already have something made to forward to me and I would just tweak it to fit my style, students, and classroom. Collaborating with my coach(es) saved me loads of time!

PLC Time

Please listen! This time is going to benefit you based on how you use it! Sure, it can be a gossip fest or time spent talking about things other than school, but I promise you that an effectively ran PLC will have you saving time and tears. Thankfully, I was able to be in buildings that had this process in place and one building had an extraordinarily strong structure to the process.

The people who roll their eyes when the administrator or coach comes in the PLC have always gotten a raised eyebrow from me. I could not understand why they were so hesitant about having a team to help support the planning process. I appreciated having leadership there to go over the building and grade-level goals. It helped hold my team accountable to have various things graded and put into the system in advance. Some days even allowed time for team scoring. I found the PLCs valuable during assessment windows to hold me accountable to get things scored and feedback to my students in time also. Having an effective agenda is critical. I found that having the agenda in place still held the group accountable for using the time wisely whether the administrator or coach was there or not. I urge you to use this time to focus on the necessary planning, standards alignment, and co-creating a structure of how-to layout a unit with your team. It will eliminate the late-night cram sessions when you are able to have a loose timeline a few weeks out. This was also a place I could bring up any student questions to prevent having to set up another meeting. Figuring out interventions when trends were being noticed between students also occurred during this time. Again, so many benefits when done right!

There are huge benefits to using this time when you have it and can hit the ground running and truly collaborate. I recall using the time left after the agenda to get worksheets, exit slip questions, and a host of other "worksheet" or presentation-type things done in advance which saved me bunches of time. Again, utilize your time and the anxiety of cram planning will lessen for you.

Specialty Times

It is all about time. I'm talking guidance, library, computer lab, and any other special event that gives you a window to get one thing done throughout your day or week. During my time in the classroom, I looked for consistent times. For example, Guidance always happened unless it was an off week. I knew my role was to help supervise. However, I also knew that with my management in place, my class was normally okay if I stepped out quickly for the restroom or to make copies. With it happening once a week or every other week I would often line up what copies I needed, run it all to the copier and get my printing started then send one of my leaders to grab everything from the lab at the end of the lesson.

During that time while I was back in the room monitoring, I also used that time to get papers graded. In my mind, that was not a break to sit back and just watch the lesson or check my phone. I wanted to be intentional about monitoring the class and still get at least two or three tasks done that I would not have to do at home, email was a priority when I had these moments. It would be the same for library time, it was consistent, I knew they would have a short lesson before being released to check out books, so I used that time to get at least one thing done. The computer lab was the same thing, I used that time to pull an extra group, or meet with students one on one to collect data. However, the key in all of this was the classroom management I had set up earlier in the year. It allowed me to have this time because my students knew what was expected of them. Yes, there were days that the class struggled, and I stepped in more, but overall, I found my year consisting of many days where I could utilize this time to be efficient. Putting this approach in place kept me busy during my contract hours, but provided relief to my task list outside of school.

Be Kind to Yourself

Lastly, my final tip is to be kind and give yourself grace. There will be days that you just have to turn off the nightly tasks. It is okay, you will survive, and your students will still have a great day of school. There are times when you need to be human, tap into your emotions, and go with what you can do. As long as you aren't staying in this mindset for long periods, you will be okay. If you do find yourself in a bad space mentally for a while, then reach out to your building leaders and those supporting you for help. It's really easy to isolate yourself and build up a wall because you expect people to know what's going on. However, if we're being honest, everyone in education has a lot on their plate and do their best to keep momentum throughout the year to genuinely help students so they may not pinpoint your struggle. We all have bad days, life events, and there are times our mental health just needs a tune-up. My advice is to always plan purposefully, but give yourself a break if a day or week even doesn't go exactly as planned. You can do this, and you were offered this job because your building administrator knows you can do this too! Trust yourself and the process.

Chapter 8
Teaching While Black: A Confessional

The Purpose

I have gone back and forth on whether to add this chapter or not as it does not have any direct strategies, but just more my experiences being a black woman in a profession where I have not seen many like me. Given the times we are in, sharing my experiences is even more critical so I am happy to share if it will help. While I know that in another area or state those dynamics and experiences could be completely different. However, I am speaking directly from being a black teacher in Iowa. I have seen more diversity in my students than I have with the people that I have worked with and my purpose of including this chapter is to show vulnerability and to share my experiences. Many have heard of "Driving While Black"; as I think of that type of experience it easily lends some of the same fears, stereotypes, and anxiety that can present itself when "Teaching While Black". My hope simply is to empower current minority teachers or leaders in this profession to continue doing what you are doing and find the praise in even the smallest of things you do each day. Along with paint the picture for non-minority educational professionals so that you will be more mindful and reflective of what your teaching partners or staff that are nonwhite might be going through as they navigate the world of education. Being mindful of your colleagues' experiences further helps you be mindful of the students you serve.

"You're our teacher? But you're black!"

I will always share this story. It is something that always comes back to memory whenever anyone asks what the most outrageous thing is that I have ever heard or seen as a teacher. It was the first day of my second year of teaching. I had brought the class to the carpet to introduce myself and give them a chance to ask me questions before jumping into learning some expectations. I stood at the front of the room and told them I would be their teacher for the year and asked them what questions they had for me before we got started. One student, a black girl that had moved to Iowa from another state raised her hand and said, "I'm not trying to be rude, but *YOU'RE* our teacher and they're going to leave you alone with us?" I laughed a little and said, "yes" and asked her why she asked that. She says, "but.... you're black...". I am thinking okay, yes that is apparent, but also was intrigued to hear more about why she asked that. I asked her, "So because I'm black I can't be your teacher?" She follows up with, "I'm just saying I've never had a black teacher before just people who have helped out in the classroom or around my school". It all made sense to me then that she was questioning something she had never experienced before; rightfully so. We all laughed as a class and many other kids agreed with her too. That ended up being one of my favorite years of teaching because I was able to take them on a journey as their first black teacher that I am sure many of them will never forget.

This moment with her always sticks in my head and that is what pushes me to go further and further in the educational world. That year is what makes me confident enough to take on opportunities of leadership and stand in rooms where there are even less people that look like me and share my voice. Even though I have always been quite the shy, quiet person 😊. I will always speak up for what is right. I want students like her to see people of color in positions that they as children, do not normally connect them with doing. If I shape one person's viewpoint or motivation to step into a role where they may be the only one from their race or culture, then I have served my purpose.

THE REAL

Full confession, I wanted to be the teacher that was my authentic self no matter who my students were. I wanted to display my preferences as a professional without making students think I had to fit into a box. My appearance was the biggest way I displayed this. My students would see me in Jordan's some days down to sandals, heels, and boots other days. My goal was to always come across as professional, whether that was dresses, dress pants, or jean days, but always be true to me. I wanted to show my students that they could be anything they wanted to be in this world. I communicated that message often whether that was with hoop earrings, pearls, straight hair, braids, long, short, or curly hair on any given day. I wanted to ensure my students saw me as a leader and role model that carried herself as a strong black woman who just so happened to be an educator that did not put herself into a box based on the opinions of others.

Winning my students over came easily compared to other stereotypes and prejudices that can be knowingly and unknowingly presented in this profession. Sure, I expected my students to not have the facts and even lack knowledge about certain things related to race. I was not naïve to the fact that a lot of my students would get a fresh cup of black history for the first time just by being in my class alone. As a black teacher, I felt the need to incorporate history throughout the year. You would often find facts up about people of all different ethnicities and I would point out key events throughout the year, not just February. This approach was further validated when I had a student who spoke up about what she had thought all the years prior about slavery. She had gone years thinking that black people wanted to come over to America. That they were here working jobs and getting paid, so she was utterly confused on what the issue was. I thanked her for being so open and willing to share because I am sure she was not the only person in that room who thought that. Yes, with my students I wanted to hear their past understandings and answer any questions they had with the hopes that as they get older, they will share their knowledge with others who do not know. So, it was not my students at all that ever brought discomfort to me in this profession. Nothing they could ask made me feel uncomfortable in those moments; they were just truly trying to learn or even unlearn prior teachings.

I found a lot of my struggles came from my past experiences related to racism; either encountered by me or someone close to me. Along with some realities from everyday encounters with non-black adults. As a black woman, I always felt that I had to prove myself to even be respected as a teacher. Whether it was true or not, it was and still is a feeling I carry with me. This feeling is a motivator for me to do well no matter what my role is. There is a level of isolation when you are the only one of your kind in certain situations. The isolation was never due to loneliness or not having support. I have always felt supported and worked with so many great educators and support staff over the years who bent over backwards to make sure I was included, celebrated, and heard. The isolation I speak of is the unending feeling day in and day out that you must prove why you are in that position versus feeling like you deserve to be there because you worked hard to get there. There were many years where I found myself having to prove myself as an educator before being accepted as a teacher. Normally, these situations played out where at the beginning of the year I would have many non-black parents give off a skeptical vibe about me being their child's teacher. Body language and facial expressions often relay the message before your mouth does-FYI. However, by the end of the year, they were singing my praises and thanking me for giving their child such a great year of learning. That period between their hesitation and them coming to full terms that I indeed was a great teacher for their child skin color aside is the isolation I speak of. A period of seeking approval from many groups you interact with not just your boss to prove to them that in the end, you are great at what you do, that type of isolation. As a minority educator, I felt the need to show and prove not only to my boss, but to my colleagues, parents, students, and even those at a distance who interacted with the educational world. It always felt like all eyes were on me to show in prove. I lost track of how many times I would go on a field trip and the person over the facility we were visiting would encounter me and my students first off of the bus and question if I was the teacher. I'd often get asked if I was a parent helper or chaperone even though my name tag clearly said the teacher. Not to mention I would have a line of students standing in front of me listening to my every direction. However, watching all of that they got parent volunteer-hmmm. I would correct those individuals. Sometimes my students would too (I had quite a few that did not play about me and would let people know I was their teacher 😊). After I would educate them on my role, the common response would always be, "Oh you're the teacher, I'm sorry I wasn't sure". My thought would always be "I wonder why?". My plan in life has always been to excel and persevere in the areas people doubt me the most and teaching proved to be one of those areas.

I recall an incident early on in my career when I was having my first round of conferences. A non-black parent, educated, with some connection and background knowledge into the education world did all, but say the words "I'm still trying to gauge if I trust your judgment and level of education". She displayed this by trying to name-drop various types of learning strategies as if I were not aware of what she was referring to. I recall her always adding the word "assuming" before telling me about various reading strategies she was having her child do at home to help strengthen their reading skills. For example, "I'm assuming you know what a running record is? Or "I'm assuming you've heard of x,y,z that is research-based to help with reading?". I would follow up to her statements by saying, "Your assumption is correct, I've used that strategy this particular way, this number of times with a different student and after reviewing the data we saw growth". Explaining the WHY or HOW I knew something was also the added layer to further back up my theory of needing to prove my expertise. It seemed I always needed to add on to conversations with certain individuals to validate my level of knowledge. It was rare that I felt like I could say "yes, I've heard of that" and that person would walk away believing in my capabilities. I learned to make my responses educational and informational to show whoever I was speaking to that I was fully capable of having a professional conversation related to my career based on data and not an assumption. Although, I cringe when I think back to some of these conversations, I can say they helped shape me into a person that was no longer reactive to the ignorance of others.

It is a known fact that there's this perception of black women being angry when they decide to be assertive or speak up for what is right. These situations have allowed me to be more cognizant of my responses in certain situations. It is never out of fear, but it stems from my need to change the narrative and prove to others that their stereotype is just that. I live my life off of the "I have everything to lose" mentality and truth be told, I do. I have worked too hard to allow anyone to get me out of character because my skin color heightens their ignorance. These encounters have taught me patience and a key life skill that it is okay to put pride and ego aside. I lost count of how many times people would say, "Wow you are so calm, soft-spoken, and patient yet your kids follow your expectations". In my mind I am thinking, yes, I do not have to be the black teacher yelling or jumping down kids' throats to get them to do something out of fear. I made the choice not to operate that way. It may work for some people, but taking on that persona would have caused me way more stress and high blood pressure from sheerly playing a role and being somebody else all those hours each day. While these types of comments may not seem offensive and being calm is a good thing, I find that the shock behind it when these statements are made equate to a person asking "Can I touch your hair" when you have a new style they have not seen before. The person on the receiving end is thinking, "why are you questioning it, just acknowledge and appreciate what it is". It is almost as if there is a surprise factor that what they are witnessing is not truly a reality they can grasp.

I do not say all of this to bash anyone, but merely as a way for people to reflect on their words and actions and how they may come across to their colleagues. The whole perception vs reality theory. The situation going down will always be interpreted differently depending on who is involved and your direct relationship with that individual. So, while it may be an omission it could stand out as insensitive to somebody else. Many of my colleagues would have probably never imagined the fear I had as a classroom teacher going to certain venues, areas, and towns for field trips. Or the battle between having their back in behavior situations with students for things I do not take offense to because it is a cultural norm to discuss things in that manner. I code switched A LOT! I made it my mission to always be open with my students about this. I always reserved one community circle early in the year to address that the Ms. Pledge they were getting was not the same Darcel that my friends and family got or the Mom that my children see. I told them that even the way I talked to my friends was not a way I would talk to my colleagues at work. Except for my one favorite para sista in the building, we'd "heeyyy girl, I see youuu, hey queen and yassss" each other to death and the students often saw this exchange and loved it. It was an exchange that came so naturally due to comfort and knowing there was another person just like me to connect with. I would explain to my students that with teaching being my professional role I needed to carry myself in that form. I also would expect them to carry themselves in a way that did not exactly mirror what they were allowed to do at home if it takes away from their professionalism. I still laugh about one day when a student called me ashy. Keep in mind I had built a great relationship with this student and knew her humor from having had lunches, talking with her at recess, and she would be one of the last students in my room picked up. So, we chatted a lot. She was often one I would remind on what was appropriate or not appropriate for school and she had no problem fixing it. She would also see me go over the top with "extra-ness" and sarcasm if I could not find lotion or Chapstick at times. So, on this particular day, we had just gone to recess and it was a Fall day, but cooler by the time we had gotten outside for recess. I didn't wear my jacket outside, but had shorter sleeves on. She says, "oooo Ms. Pledge your arms ashy" and we both start laughing. I am joking around with her telling her she should have brought her lotion outside to share, rubbing my arms, blowing into my hands trying to reduce the ash, but the ash is growing bigger ha-ha. She then ran and told a few other kids close to us who wanted to know why we were laughing. The next time I look up, another teacher (non-black) has her pulled to the side. Her demeanor had changed, and she almost looked annoyed. The student came back over to me and said the other teacher had heard her telling the other kids and told her how disrespectful she was being. Also, that if she continued it would be a write-up for disrespect and defiance. I was so caught off guard because in my mind the term ashy is universally known in a black household. You're either ashy or you're not in mind. I told the student no worries I knew she was joking, but that was also a lesson that other people might not know when she is joking. The teacher that pulled her to the side came over by me and said what he had told her about being disrespectful to adults. I had to clarify and let him know that I took no offense to what she was saying because it was a cultural connection to that student that we both found humor in. Which that teacher said he did not know that and did go and apologize. Thankfully, this situation got resolved, but I think of so many instances where our minority students come in with built-in cultural habits that are hard for them to magically break once the school year starts. Often it gets them off on the wrong foot with their teacher because it is viewed as disrespect. Being a black teacher there are things I can "tolerate" more and work with students more on because I know the context and experiences behind it. Instead of writing them up, I viewed it as an educational moment of what's appropriate whereas other colleagues may be intolerant and choose to do an office referral every time. The balance in these interactions must be prevalent to understand our students and the people we work with that do not look like you. Some students must be taught how to treat their teachers and peers and that cannot happen if their mannerisms are immediately punished versus addressed. Teachable moments are key, especially early on when wanting to build relationships with your students.

This again, is another topic I could go on and on about having lived and continuing to live through it. Every day was not a walk in the park even if it so happened to be a good day in my classroom. I often found myself reiterating certain things to colleagues about students or having one on one conversations with students of color on how to handle their own experiences with other teachers or peers that did not look like them. While I never had racist comments said to me directly by a student or parent, I did have situations where there were students who would use certain terms towards other students. It was hurtful because often it would be a non-black student that I had a great relationship with saying these things out of anger to peers that looked like me over a simple misunderstanding. Having those discussions that saying something like that to another student held the same weight as saying it to me was the typical conversation we would have. Most of those students saying those words used them in anger and it was clear they had learned it in other settings as an appropriate way to express their anger. So, that was a big battle I wanted to tackle. Which goes back to why my motto was always "You don't have to like me, but you will respect me".

Some years my class needed more teaching in this area than others. Those were the things I needed to keep an eye and ear for. I knew the students weren't saying it in front of me, so I needed to be strategic in my community circles, and community-building efforts to communicate that hate was not tolerated in any form. Each week in my planning I always strived to have a representation of all types of people in the learning texts, videos, and activities we would have. I would allow students to rap, dance, or bring in cultural visitors to show them that there are people in the world doing great things that are not always white. While I felt it was my duty I began thinking, "It is really?" Why must I be the black teacher bringing the culture into education? I would always reassure myself that what I was doing meant something and it would make a lasting impact on my kids. So, among doing all of the regular duties as an educator, my skin tone pushed me to think outside of the box to reach all students and help them connect with diversity. Which is not a focus in a lot of other teacher's classrooms that I can attest to.

I would love to go on and on about my experiences in this area, but I will save that for another time and place. My honest feedback and advice would be to see color. I was always confused when I would sit in different pieces of training and hear, "You should not see color, all of your students are the same and should be treated the same". I realize there have been many years of absent equity etiquette that I am happy to see now coming back into play. So, see color. That way you know who you are dealing with and what tools you may need to put in your educational tool kit to reach all students and staff you may work with. Whether you have a minority student in your class or not; some emphasis should be placed on representation throughout the school year. In my room we talked about all history. I remember finding pictures from key points in history and having students do remakes of those pictures with me and writing about those events in the form of an Instagram post. Something quick, engaging, and unique to spark their interest and learn about things outside of the standard textbook. We would do inventor projects where I would cover the typical faces of black history in my modeling and encourage my students to investigate other figures from history to share with their peers. I would always provide a list of names of other diverse figures that made contributions to this world that they would have never known about. There are ways to shake up and provide representation to symbolize unity within your classroom.

As for your black colleagues, my best advice is to just be understanding and have empathy. On any giving day, your non-white colleague is not only coming to work with the weight of their job role, but the weight of the world, its' prejudices, bias, stereotypes, and systemic limitations in just about every other facet of life. I did not want someone to act or talk differently with me because of my race. Nor did I expect anyone to walk on eggshells or feel the need to only have "black conversations" around me. I always felt welcomed to staff outings and it was my preference, out of comfort, which things I would attend or choose not to attend. Sometimes it would be a matter of what was going on in the world at that time, the location of the event, or how the day had been in general. I would take all these factors into account before determining if I would have the mental capacity to attend. This had absolutely nothing to do with my specific colleagues at the time, but a mere in-the-moment personal preference.

An important note: NO, your black colleague does not need you to have "sister girl" moments with her to connect during those times that she may be operating at a level of sheer black girl magic to get through a staff presentation or speak up for students who are falling through the cracks. Just a listening ear and being mindful of the freedoms your privilege allows you to have more accessibility to mentally, emotionally, and physically is a great start. Some of my best and most appreciated conversations from non-black colleagues were after I may have shared something and a simple "thank you for sharing, I am now informed" followed. Keeping a team mindset and having each other's back and being open to learning is my key look for when determining which colleagues were in my corner versus just standing in my circle.

Full confession though, I loved teaching in the classroom as an African American woman. I felt most at home and not judged when I was with my students. People are not born racist. I saw this year after year with students who did not look like me, but genuinely loved me as their teacher. I created great bonds and collaborative relationships with so many great educators. With all this, there were and still are many moments where I felt out of place in the educational world. I pushed through with the understanding that what I was doing and felt would be worth it. My mentality always was, as long as my students could see someone like me at least once in their educational career, teaching while black would be all worth it.

Chapter 9
It's a Wrap: I Said All of That to Say This

Keeping It 100

Teaching is hard. Being a part of the educational world, in general, is hard. Being underappreciated in a vital role is hard. Having people outside of the field make decisions about your work is hard! Ultimately, doing the extra necessities to set your students up for success is hard. One thing I know is that through all of this, educators have found a way to make magic happen in the lives of their students. You will find that emotions you have never tapped into are suddenly being awakened. It all becomes motivation to become a greater version of yourself for the ones looking up to you. No matter the age or content area, there is something to be taken from how you operate as a teacher. Teaching is not about having everything figured out. It is not a one size fits all scenario. You will find that you need to shift, rock, and roll with whatever circumstances that come at you during that day. You can plan, but realize you are navigating in the moment making decisions that are going to benefit your students every day. It is okay to have bad days. It is okay to be in the heart of a lesson and shift gears. There is not a universal rule as to what great teaching should look like. However, there are people out there doing amazing things that encompass what great teaching is. I found that the things that made me nervous about teaching were the things I made the most growth in because the challenge excited me even through the hesitation. It is okay to be uncomfortable in a situation and go back to the drawing board and think about how to address it later. I had a few situations like that myself where partner work was not going as planned or a whole group movement activity did not go as planned. At that moment, the only thing I could do was stop the activity have the students do something different and think about a better way to roll the activity out. Or decide that it was an activity that maybe my students could not handle that year. Both decisions are ok if it makes sense for your students.

FULL CONFESSION (REALITY CHECK)

I may strike a nerve here, but in the best interest of students, so be it. ANYONE in education listen up! If there is not a passion in you when you think about a career in education, bypass this career field. There are too many people at risk should you choose to join this field and be mediocre or do it to get by. Teaching is not a "get by" job. Even the most prepared have challenges at times. The risk of coming into this role without the passion to serve, motivate, and inspire puts your students, families, and building staff at a disadvantage. What will happen is eventually the job will become too much and you find yourself clinging to justifications of why you are just mediocre. In the end, your students suffer the most. I have been around teachers like this, and their lack of passion for the role often walks into staff meetings before they physically do.

Full confession, if you want to be recognized for everything you do, hang up your emotions when you leave your classroom each day, or have your handheld throughout this entire process, then teaching may not be for you. Teaching requires a balance between collaborating effectively with others and trusting and pushing yourself enough independently to see great things happen for your students. There may be days that roll into nights because you need to execute something just right. There is a high probability your lunch break a few times a week will consist of multi-tasking where you're eating, making copies, checking in with a student, but it's worth it! If it dismisses you from sitting in on a negative, rumor mill lunch with others then you are winning by choosing to multitask. You will have students and families that are not able to chip in and help with events and activities happening. This is all okay! The passion comes from an intrinsic motivation to change the lives of those many students coming in and out of your classroom. Anything tangible is just an additive. One year could change a student's entire outlook on their educational experience. You owe them the best version of you. If you are finding yourself referring to students as "those kids" or "that group" or "this class" and it stops you from giving your all to accommodate them then again, I urge you to reconsider your career path. The future is dependent on you receiving each student and finding ways to build them up better than they arrived to you. Being a parent, I would always check myself by thinking, "Would I be okay if my child's teacher was operating this way". I could not see myself holding my child's teacher to a standard that I was not willing to adhere to either. If you are struggling in the role, write down the pros and cons. See if those cons are related to a knowledge gap that seeking guidance might help you fix.

No lie, any coach you are given starting out is going to be one of the best assets you can have. I remember being in those moments where it may have taken an extra prep time for me to meet or have someone come observe and I sometimes got irritated. However, it wasn't until my third year that I realized I HAD to start putting into a place a lot of things my mentor pushed me on, but it would be by my own motivation this time. I missed having that consistent voice and feedback, but also knew that because I sucked it up, had those meetings, and did work focused on my students and practice, I was a better teacher because of it and could implement changes. It helped me not be scared to ask for help when I found areas that just were not quite clicking right in my room. Whether it is a building coach or someone else assigned from your district, utilize that person to refine your craft early on and you will see major improvements! There is a method to the madness, I promise you! If you find your list does not indicate a gap related to enhancing a skill then consider if this role fits your lifestyle, beliefs, and goals. Do you really believe all students can achieve? Our students are far too valuable to have a wreck less adult behind the wheel when it comes to their education.

FINAL THOUGHTS

I have always said that my life could be summed up using a series of Maya Angelou quotes and that statement still holds true. My email tag line continues to be my favorite quote by her, "People will forget what you said, people will forget what you did, but people will never forget how you made them feel". I carry that quote with me now everywhere. It is the main thing that makes me stop and put everything into perspective. To me, that quote does not mean I should be a yes woman in every situation. It means being an advocate and leaving people with an experience that evokes some sort of emotion and inspiration. Or helping them realize their significance. If a firm conversation with a student made that student feel like they needed to examine their decision-making moving forward, then in my mind I had done my job. If I can help someone feel empowered, then I have succeeded.

To be a teacher means there are highs, lows, demands, challenges, successes, failures, happy times, and opportunities for reflection. My first year of teaching taught me this. When it comes to teaching it is about your mindset. In the words of Henry Ford, "Whether you think you can or you think you can't, you're right". So, as you tackle this year of education, I hope that you find your purpose and mix it with some passion, hope, and motivation. Find the good people in your building that boost morale and think positively. Your kids deserve it, and you deserve this mindset as you embark on a journey that can save someone's future or put them on a different path.

To sum up everything, my goal here has been to share my experiences coming into this field as a late bloomer and give some advice while providing clear examples of what worked for me. Again, I am no expert, but I found myself able to adjust to this role rather quickly as I started doing these other duties not officially assigned to me in my role. To this day, I will always keep with me that I impacted many students who still reach out and thank me for our educational experience together. It was not easy being in Ms. Pledge's classroom, there were some high expectations, but it was worth it. My joy came from seeing students who had no spark suddenly brighten up because we were doing a project or activity that interested them.

As I close, I want to leave you with what became my education and even life motto by none other than the late great Maya Angelou. "My mission in life is not merely to survive, but to thrive and to do so with some passion, some compassion, some humor, and some style". I urge you to thrive and make this the best year yet! You have it in you, now execute your greatness!

About the Author

Darcel was born in Cedar Rapids, Iowa in 1985. She graduated from Washington Highschool in 2004. She went on to earn her Bachelor of Arts degree from the University of Northern Iowa in 2008 where she studied elementary education. After taking some time to explore roles in the corporate world and raise her first born, Darcel obtained a Master of Arts degree in 2012 from the University of Northern Iowa in Performance & Training Technology. Shortly after, Darcel took a leap and returned to her true passion, education. From that moment on, she has committed herself to being a forward thinking, outside of the box educator. She recently received her Master of Science degree in Educational Leadership from Drake University in 2019. Darcel currently serves in a leadership role as a coach for beginning teachers. This is Darcel's second book published. Her first book, "Laila's Life: Journeys to Building Good Character" was released in 2014 with a black female lead character encouraging children from all walks of life to make positive choices and be the best versions of themselves no matter what. Darcel has a love for writing that stems back to her years as an elementary student. Writing is her freedom of expression and her hope is that everyone that encounters her work walks away with the message and motivation to impact the future generation. Thanks for your support!

Thank you SO much for reading! ~Darcel

Made in the USA
Middletown, DE
23 May 2021

40270011R00059